Three or Four Hills
and a Cloud

Wesleyan Poetry Program: VOLUME 106

Three or Four Hills and a Cloud

and a Cloud

Robert Farnsworth

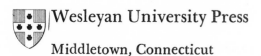

Wesleyan University Press

Middletown, Connecticut

The author would like to thank Daniel Halpern, George Colt, Stanley Plumly, and Kevin Murphy for their advice and encouragement.

Grateful acknowledgment is made to the editors of the following periodicals, in which some of the poems in this book first appeared:

The American Poetry Review: "The Whale"; *Canto:* "The Poem of the Bath"; *Carolina Quarterly:* "Natural History," "Poem Timed to an Egg"; *The Georgia Review:* "Blaming The Swan"; *Ironwood:* "Sestina"; *The Ohio Review:* "Meditation That Concludes On an Atlantic Beach"; *Poetry:* "Music for Piano and Electrical Storm"; *Poetry Northwest:* "Groceries," "A Man Mistaken For Pretty Boy Floyd"; *Shenandoah:* "Novella"; *The Southern Review:* "Grenouillère," "Speech to a Dog"; *Three Rivers Poetry Journal:* "Pegasus"

"If there were" takes its title and opening lines from John Berryman's Dream Song #385. "Douce Ame" is the title of a medieval soup recipe that calls for "parsley, hyssop, sage, savoury, and other good herbs." "Study for a Life of Perdix" is based on Ovid's account of his transformation in Book VIII of *The Metamorphoses.* "A Lover's Quarrel With the World" takes its title from Robert Frost's poem, "The Lesson For Today." The title of the collection comes from Wallace Stevens's poem, "Of The Surface of Things."

Published by Wesleyan University Press, Middletown, Connecticut
Manufactured in the United States of America
First Edition

Photograph facing title page by John Theilgard

Library of Congress Cataloging in Publication Data
Farnsworth, Robert, 1954-
  Three or four hills and a cloud.

  (Wesleyan poetry program; v. 106)
  I. Title. II. Series.
PS3556.A725T5   811'.54   82-4932
ISBN 0-8195-2108-6   AACR2
ISBN 0-8195-1108-0 (pbk.)

for Georgia
and to the memory of
Elizabeth M. Farnsworth and Robert L. Gibson

Contents

In my room, the world is beyond my understanding;
But when I walk I see that it consists of three or four hills
and a cloud.

WALLACE STEVENS

I

Rubric

A window is reflected in my tea.
By the time it's cold a dozen clouds
will pass beyond the red peripheries
of the cup, the way faces that crowd
my sleep vanish from backlit membranes
in the skull. The sun will sink
on the garden outside: inflamed
peppers, bitter hearts of turnip, wrinkled
chard. Red sky at night, red sky at morning—
I think of Percival's moated Mars,
or the first red cells Leeuwenhoek saw.
The long clouds crossing my cup warn me
to love the blush that fades under the loving eye,
the hard weather we bear in our blood to survive.

Groceries

A rich gray light has settled in the trees
as I walk out of the market, heading home.
The sky would play me false if I thought rain,
or even wind. Instead the light refers me
back to dark gymnasium windows in December.
Trembling on my staff I'm Joseph again, rehearsing
entrances with a girl who smells like boiled corn
and old clothes. Outside father is killing
time in the old black Chevy with wings.

These hours the color of dull nickel
have become a kind of rhyme.
Between them I'm anyone I can invent,
on my way to extravagant success or early doom.
Afternoons like this keep me honest, like a clock.

So this is what they meant by "man's estate"—
an indigo eggplant, celery,
cod fillets, a breadstick,
butter, limes, and a small bottle of gin
with a yellow label.
It's as if I'd taken the wrong bag.
Even these old mansards seem suddenly
unfamiliar, the light bankrupting their casements.
To really get lost I need only think
of the world that's hidden behind the groceries:

long striped fields wavering in the heat,
a blue forest swept with snow, lush fog
on the Banks, and a bell moaning.
Whatever's derived, distilled, despoiled
returns, as surely as the tarnished skins of fish
go back to the soil, as the earth works in silence
at the small futures of leaves, as I will find
an excuse to spend the last few coins in my pocket.

Today I add this year to my catalogue of autumns.
Inside a small voice keeps saying
Become, become.
Slowly I come to understand directions—
climbing the stairs with the meal
I've planned for tonight, a first step.
Here, in this bag, these
are some of my choices.

Coloring Book

The strawberries lie in a dish of cream.
The man has chosen them, pulled
their green crowns off and halved
their whole red hearts with a knife.

Feast your eyes, he says. He knows
to seek the world at its ripest.
But the child, confronted with page after page
of empty outlines, is puzzled.

If she learns that in April strawberries
are tiny green replicas of strawberries,
does she ignore what her bitter tongue
has told her, and color them green?

She turns the page. The blue egg at the foot
of the oak outside is her secret. It is empty.
She wonders what left it, and if it lived.
From where she sits by the window,

the yard with the oak and her bicycle seems
smaller than it is. In the coloring book
there is nothing like her life but one hatched
egg. She colors it blue. The man says that once

he rowed home under clouds with a flounder
that swam in a bucket of gravel and water.
While he watched, it colored itself like stones
and bits of shale. He wished he'd had a bucket

of quartz so he'd have gotten a fish
like a rusting moon. But dead it turned an evil
umber anyway. They share the strawberries. He
tells her about a Frenchman who lived on a flatboat

every summer, painting the river Seine, the sky
within the river, the water flowers and the quays.
This, the man says, was an act of love. Thinking
of love, and the crayons spread across the table,

he is happy with the world. Things he tells her,
have an order we don't yet understand. Even
the traffic lights turn green to yellow to red all
night, though no one is there to obey them.

How Spring Gets in the Window

Warm you think
the way a hawk thinks
something moved there.

The wind's thin gesture
in the curtain leaves
no trace, a perfect accident
to close the grueling cinema:
mute wrens, rocky clouds,
snow that for months
has gleamed on the window.

Turning in the moment
swung open with this touch,
the mild light looks in
as if it had been expecting
you, and not the reverse.
It has the proximity
of a thumb on a mirror.

Shadows boil on the wall.
Each passage in the street below
bulges through the window.

The first star climbs
toward deeper sky.
Slowly the house inflates
with sweet dark air
and floats among the trees.

Someone has just set out
to join you for the evening.

Fantasia on a Line of Donne

Good is as visible as green:
bottle green morning after,
fear's insidious yellow
bleed into the lonesome
blues, what smokes but will not
catch and burn, the strange air
of leaves before thunder,
when the light's as neutral
as the taste in the mouth
promising violent illness:
green caught in the act,

or the blameless green
of young translucent perch,
a baseball diamond illuminating
your doze beside the radio,
the whispering chambers
street lamps make in the elms,
fifteen emerald acres of unripe
oats at sunrise. Good is as
visible as green. Turn this
new leaf over, wake and rise
while the radium clockface is

still the only light, believe
in your thought until it thinks
about green, all that rumpled
green tucked into pockets, all the good
green clover in the graveyard.
Accept that whatever happens
fulfills a wish made long ago
in an innocent age, by nothing
even so complex as a cell.
Smell the sharp green
of the pickle barrel burst

on a city street, but don't
suppose it's all been decided
in advance. You must still choose
or be chosen. Let every green
returned to the eye remind you,
deny you camouflage. Walk
among hundreds of snow-crusted
pines, bathe at evening
in the certain tide. Good
is as visible as green.

Speech to a Dog

Don't think I'm out of line
I know my part—
procurer of bones
opener of vile cans

the slow runner panting
exhilarated with chasing you
for the stick
in your grinning jaws

the fall guy for your feints
and whining in the morning.

You do not run me too hard
demand the impossible of me.
I am grateful for this
as you are for having a name
to approach.

Sometimes we have sung together
when the pitch stuck in your throat.

So how can you sit there blinking
puzzled with my laughter
the severed rubber arm of a doll
clenched in your teeth?

You lope off, nose down, bored with me.
Below the knee the world
lives another life.

Natural History

Learn never to say there is no such thing,
because if you must, there is
or was. The thought of 'walking the earth'
discovered huge footprints in the eelgrass.

•

When they found the bones they were a map
of the shape they once supported. A child straddles
a femur twice her size. The skull looks on,
a tiny white summit.

•

One leaf can suggest a mysterious tree.
What can be said about the taste of the ancient yellow fruit?
If I said the seeds were tiny, you could believe
as you wished, about anything, dead or alive.

•

I can only go back so far. Once there was
a horse the size of a dog. It was useless,
and disappeared while our ancestors observed
the mottled necks of giraffes, lengthening.

•

Again the deer feels the antlers shake loose,
splitting from the skull root.
Under the smoked drum of the ice the carp wake up
to this, as I might to a rattle of chairs overhead.

•

And what are the wolves? In the night's blue snow
the wolves are a circle of eyes. In the early morning
a lifting of black lips. Near the cracked stream,
a sudden bloodshot flurry.

•

I save two turtles from the traffic. Where do they think
they're going? A turtle in an old schoolroom was empty,
smelled like a riverbed drying in the sun.
A tiny gold latch would open its belly.

•

With patience, could we have bred a bird
large enough and willing to carry us? How much barley
or beef would it have required? The great black scythes
of its wings would have combed continents.

•

If I could I would float first
in the huge rib cage of the brontosaurus.
I would try to think for both ends at once.
The four soles of my feet would be tender.

•

A spider climbs the dry air beside my bed.
It has its reasons.
I think for a long time of sleeping upside down in the dark,
before I think that perhaps while I sleep, it does not.

•

I wake with a thought. A wish.
A need to know I've been forgiven,
to see, not even a yard ahead of me,
a sudden blossom of dust, to bend and find the spent bullet.

Poem Timed to an Egg

Already it rattles in the pot,
while outside wedges
of sunlight merge
and disband on the grass.
I put down my book
and watch a portly neighbor
hammering in his yard,
the shoulder of his red shirt working
like a jaw among the leaves.
The sound arrives late, between
the blows, the last more final
than his satisfaction
with the straightly driven nail.
These things take time.
Then they're forgotten,
as if a priest or judge
or genie said:
It is done. So be it.
Time takes its time with us
no matter what's discovered
while we wait.
This morning, for example,
I found the crowd of early
poppies wilted with rain.
Now my neighbor builds
a shelter for his seedlings,
and I rinse a boiled egg
to eat later in the day.

And though we both suppose
we have altered the future,
there is really nothing
to it yet. In the oak
a thrush is already hard at work
confusing its cries
with those of the children
beginning their mutable games.

Meditation that Concludes
on an Atlantic Beach

I don't think I'll ever shake this coast,
no matter where we settle finally—
the old seaboard that father patrolled
while his navy wife alone learned how to curse
in the heat of Charleston, South Carolina.
All I was ever told was that mother burned
some meals there and doubled her smoking
while quickly I grew inside her.
I imagine those nine months from August of '53
as an impossible stillness, the reign
of mother's fear. Evenings topside
with fragments of her letters in his head,
father would stare out across his future,
a kind of bronze age the ship cut steadily
into. More than once the summer sky
must have gone pale green and lit with vivid
deltas of lightning. She trembled, talked back
to the radio, gathered up another wasted
hand of solitaire. Three seasons they waited—
mother for father out at sea, father
for mother barely twenty, and both of them
for a stranger.

•

It can take three days for a log in the shallows
to work free of the combers and beach for good,
or a year for the sand to bevel a bottleneck smooth.

•

In the wasp-waisted silver pitcher
on the bookshelf, the bedroom ceiling
becomes a white octagon. We could not pass
through the slivers of door or window.

•

In bed at six
our bodies take on
the color of dusk.
Why do we whisper
in our empty house,
why do we tremble so?
Your smile flares up
at me, as if struck
upon this secret.

●

Suppose our love,
so carefully engineered
in the dark keeps
ghosts in their graves.
Suppose that on the edge
of our sweet exhaustion
the numina we've ignored
are waiting,
waiting

●

I don't know how long the hermit crab
has lived in the shell I coax him from.
I ask him, what's to be hoped from a child?

●

I read: perhaps a mother's crying or laughter
affects the unborn child. There is so much
we don't know.

We know how she will be called.

●

How little we can say with certainty,
even now after twenty-five years.
What little we can promise
we've promised each other.
Who will know
where what we did left off
and what happened to us began?

•

On the beach tonight years before your birth
I squint out to the furthest whitecap
gnashing on the bar.
And into the brunt of the wind
I say your name again and again

until it sounds as it will to me.

Novella

Neither memory nor the odor left from tonight's belated rain
would come close enough to be named. Nothing in the dark
window edged with silver leaves would bear apostrophe.
Waking up, his stomach drops down cold at the sight
of someone keeping vigil in the rocker, before he decides
it is only his jacket, slung over the chair beneath a vase.
No one is there to tell him if this darkness is something
woken into, or something incompletely woken from. One hand
has gone to sparks under his chin; he shakes it
as someone at a bedside snaps a thermometer's silver down—
the better to rise. His skin feels hot and dry,
his whole body inscrutably indisposed. The single light
left slanting in the kitchen makes a wholesome invitation
of the walnut doors left severally ajar, like some Flemish
interior scene that would draw you past the flowers on a table,
down a hall and into a room where a thickset woman is slicing
a wedge of cheese. All this he has the leisure and refinement
to remark at three in the morning, while a siren spirals
away into the hills. But if his illness, real or imagined,
or his cultivation is to be of interest, he must be made
whole, all of a sympathetic piece in this hushed room, as if
a completely plausible life had led him precisely here
to wake inside your head. So take yourself in silence
up the stairs and undress. Turn down the bed and recline,
slowly so as to let the cool sheets envelop your bare back.
You will be comforted by this, but not completely.
Think of him as he left you today on the bridge, his long
coattails stylized with wind. Think of what he knows
that is precious to you, that he will forever withhold.
Most of all remember how the rain steamed on the pavement,
and the faint perfume of magnolia rising in the leaves.

Grenouillère
or the princess and the frog

Through the still surface I see
your face close to mine, searching itself.

Perhaps a blue dragonfly trembles
near your nose or dusk seeks out
the various edges of your hands and hair,
tumbling fabulous shadows over me.

Your words, small gestures full of silence,
seem to push the casual currents
through the weeds. Can you see through
the uncertain sheet where water

thins into air? I am down here.
Fine threads of light turn gold and green.
Pike and the dangerous mossy turtle
lurk under this black branch—

near where you dropped your glasses
one night from the canoe. These remain
with me like sunken archways. You never
wear them near water anymore.

So I am not familiar with what you
look like half the day. But I remember
a night on the pier when we decided
to fish with a flashlight, and you sat

with the light coming up between your thighs—
the tangle of fish line on your lap
was nearly silver. And I remember from out
on the lake, fearing for one of us

when your laughter drifted from the forest
out to me. You made maps
of everything. The trees amazed you;
music hung in their long dark vaults.

But I am no longer there. I am refracted, I wobble,
shrink from daylight. Each time your face
has suddenly, spitefully dispersed, I say
I will not be afraid. Night shares moonlight

with the swimmer. I wish only that I could
wake on some Baltic shore with sunrise
slicing through the dark nest
of my enormous wicker chair.

A Man Mistaken for Pretty Boy Floyd

At seven the August clouds flame
out of the prairie. He stands
beside the miniature chalet,
near the water hazard
and the Chinese bridge,
watching his niece's ball pop out
the door and down the ramp,
roll and come to rest beside the flag.
She plays with a terrible pleasureless
nonchalance, as if ten years of visits
here had suddenly produced in her
pity or impatience. Perhaps she is too old
to hear, or not yet old enough.
But she'll listen, as always
trimming the end of his cigar
with the pearly knife she loves,
she'll listen:

marathon dancers reveling
in Madison Square Garden,
long brown freights slack
in derelict yards, huddles
called over smoldering ashcans
in the cold, the radio that was
deaf and optimistic. Sometimes sitting
by the tiny office, watching the players
laughing or the lovers quarreling,
he wonders how anything came of it—
sometimes people seem diminished
just for having survived, like the small
game left in a forest where the nobler
beasts have died. The thick stubbled
flesh of his hands looks strange to him.

He left a patch of skin
on the cold freight to Arkansas
the night he let go and jumped,
but it's long since healed over.
How much will she believe?
The bluesmen smoked all night
in Kansas City, and in the room
by the tracks, cages of light
swung across the ceiling at 2:40,
and the windows shook while twenty cars
passed by. One night he woke at 2:45—
the dark door was roaring still,
gun-butts and voices shouting
Open up Pretty Boy!
We know you're in there!

It will take years for her
to understand what he won't say—
that when his alibi was proven,
and in the dusty light of the station office
the G-men's faces fell
and there was silence
he'd looked at his hands,
almost as disappointed
as they were in their wrinkled vests
and shoulder-holsters, dead wrong.
Then she will know
how he remembered for years
and envied the man who drove off
with himself into the dark
and got away.
20,000 came to Sallisaw
when they finally laid him down.

She leans over her last putt
and he calls out—Supper when you sink it!
She will believe him always,
sometimes for his sake, and sometimes
for the story's, even though his wife
will say it never happened, even though
at sundown in an Oklahoma graveyard,
the tall grass ripples over the stones,
denying everything.

Pegasus

Knee deep in black water and foam
the children struggle with the hull,
rein it upwind, lugging on halyard
and sheet to set the sail. Tucked
aboard, they bear out,
the phosphors gleaming in their wake.

In the bathroom the darkness is cool
lavender and witch hazel. The woman holds
her breasts and waits, watching the moon's
rim glint through the tissue of clouds.
She thinks how their eyes, shut there
on their pillows, tremble with all they dream
    they're touching.

The children slide toward deeper water
from which they could never swim,
toward the center of the dark, until it sounds
off the sail, a pig-iron tower looming
over them, breathing with barnacles,
hatches rimed shut with guano and salt.

Up close the beacon is blinding. The children
become after-images and their laughter
sounds like birds as one by one they climb
into the tower, fearless, taking hold
of the brass clappers to compose
their one-note allegros or silence.

The house creaks. In the weak light she sees
herself move in the mirror down the hall.
The dogs shuffle and settle again below.
There is something taking hold of her,
an absence, a departure she cannot trace.
Her own breath is what she is just beginning
    to hear.

Study for a Life of Perdix

I was first afraid when I heard him
fill a bath for me in the dark, his
long spade fingers decanting the oils.
The water was so hot it itched
in the small of my back. I smelled
of cloves and olives for a week.

One afternoon I watched the waves
unfurl dark banners of seaweed
an instant before they fell upon
the beach. Boredom made me cut
a stick of driftwood with the fish spine
I had found. It was my first invention.

His eyes glowed when he saw it,
and the sticks and string that drew
perfect circles in the sand. Visitors
fussed over my toys, talked
of forging them in iron. They didn't see
how strange the pale dust of wood was.

I should have known for certain
when he found mother and me in a grove
of olive trees, staring at the stars
together, whispering. I know now
what he thought. She asked him to watch
the moon rise with us, but he would not.

At sunrise on Pallas Athena's day
we climbed to the roof of her temple.
My insides quaked and fluttered.
With one hand on my shoulder, he pointed
down to the Agora, full of bright flags
and plumes of smoke, and out across the sea

where the plum line of horizon was melting
in the heat. What nerve it took while
the goddess watched, how gentle his hand was
guiding me, how delicate the pressure
between my shoulders, as if I could swim in air
if only I believed in him. I never reached the ground.

Sherlock Holmes in Byzantium

For years you divined what exactly happened
from imbalanced footprints, weightless
flecks of ash. In this kingdom deduction
becomes a kind of prophecy. Under the twilit
apse solutions of mercury and blood
simmer in their vials. Everything
turns to gold: domes, dust, fire, the ripping
Bosporus, the flung-out vault of the sky.

The goldfinch cocks its head while you tend
the bees and delphiniums. Your nose, under
its last disguise of gauze, suggests the sullen
ghost you have become. Boredom never suited you.
Consider what was to blame for the miseries
you unravelled—was it greed, or poverty
of spirit, or the age itself? You were what
the age demanded. Now, out of nature, sympathize
with poor Professor Presbury, who hoped to find
his youth in the blood of the baboon.

The Christ in the *Deësis* over your bed
has a criminal look, his fingers curled in a high sign.
The comedy of manners has lasted, though borders
and prayers have changed. The sun now sets
on all manner of venereal empires. Your interest
in prophecy will grow—there are infinite
pictures to be made of the stars that burn
in your blue window. Who will let you know
when eternity has ended?

An Italian minister was killed today, Holmes.
They riddled him and stuffed him in a car and got away.
Nobody knows where they will strike next,
nobody knows where they hide. What good
can come of this? In the stereopticon your old
furniture clings to the rugs. The cheval glass
is empty, the Persian slipper, empty,
and the turn of the century has turned
back to fire and earth.

If there were

a middle ground
between things and the soul
it would be here
where the water idles
in the yellow reeds,
where the hollow shellfish
compile to rot.
I'm always bringing
my speeches here,
but nothing said this morning
will further my life.

Cordgrass
searocket
moonsnail
mussel
Inventory doesn't hold
the shore in place,
any more than the names
I've given my troubles
answer them.

The tide has left
the stones in thin casts
of frost, as if this beach
could be recreated
in a place far north.
In a fragment of ice
hang ribbons of sea lettuce,
crushed slate, a crab
the size of a narrowed pupil.

Suppose the thrown stone

were to wake in midflight.
Would it not think it was
meant to fly?

My white breath rises
lifting nothing,
proof enough of all
I have become.

Half a mile out
the clammers stand in their skiffs,
working their rakes
like semaphores.
Sounds of tackle
and a radio come to me
clear as if I sat beside them.

This morning
before the wind comes
I have no need of promises,
of reflection.
The world is keen
And unanswerable.
A gull jumps
from a rock, drags
its feet on the blinding
water at first,

and pumps into the air.

Solstice

Twilight lengthens and coppers
the floor beneath the window.
I sit thinking about what supper
will consist of, did I forget to wax

the left rear hubcap this afternoon,
who will my team's pitcher
be tonight? The damp smell of mown
grass drifts through the screens.

In the red and white trumpets
of the flowers I've no name for,
the crickets are again impossibly
loud. This evening the opacities

of contentment won't allow me
a view beyond or back into my life.
Yet they are almost savory,
these trifling concerns of mine,

something, I suppose, like the secrets
children keep, waiting up for company
in their pajamas on the porch, while
stars climb to their places in the sky.

Douce Ame

Just after midnight I come downstairs, pausing
to make you wonder what's on my mind.
There is nothing now—the lights are going out
all over town and so are mine. There is
nothing but the motive to make you ask
and something like hunger. You're wrapped
in a blanket, reading at the center of the weak
lamp's pool of light. I want to tell you how
I can't rid words of their weight, how fluency
lingers out of reach like a marvelous odor
misapprehended by the tongue and washed away,
how years have passed, and still I have not
restored a single prince to his rightful throne.
I kiss you instead, and long after you're asleep
I stay in the kitchen, on the pretext of making
a grocery list. Instead I take spice bottles
down from the cabinet one at a time—basil,
cilantro, cumin, tarragon, bay—and fill my head
with their fragrances, as I would with sad airs
for strings. Gently then, without a word,
I reopen the steady silence to suggestion.

II

The Poem of the Bath

for my wife

That first night I woke in lamplight. Poised
on one leg in the pantry, the other stretched back
through your robe to hold off the door,
you searched the dark top shelf with your hands.

I don't remember what you were after, bottle
or box or fruit, but that image of you
from a drowsy spring night has lasted, though the robe
has gone to rags. Now against the white window
you nearly take on its form again,

bearing in your gestures every elegance
or pratfall I will ever love in you. I am the keeper
of snowflakes, each a different picture for a biography
of us. In one it's so hot we've doffed our clothes
and the high clouds shred in the sunlight.

In another we lie in bed in Philadelphia, making up
conversations for shadows across an alley. This adds up
to the vaguest kind of history, suspect,
but luminous as an enormous moon lifting slowly
out of a hill. We naturally assume the rest of its shape

before it emerges. This morning gondolas of melon
glisten before us and black sparrows strewn across
the window disappear. The light rises
out of the snow. Elephants and butterflies
in the Sunday papers will provide the substance

and color of a dream ten years from now. In the tub,
with the bubbles drifted around us, you watch me sadly,
as if you'd die my maid. There is more to this than fondness,
more than the gentle flexion of a smooth thigh that undoes me,
for if I claim to bear within my heart a bracelet of pearls

for you, you know me well enough to laugh, to say I must have
swallowed it on a dare. And I know, watching you rise
from the bath in the cloudy mirror, how colorful wings
will emerge from our recollections, and wait patiently to dry.

The Truth

Father, could you bring back
the field for me? Was there
a foam of clover, or did I sketch that
in some later embellishment,
claiming—I can see it now.
I can't, quite. Now if it mattered,
I'd have to rely on you to know
what happened, as once I relied
on you to know what would,
but I don't ask. You've told me
that at three I climbed out of the crib,
toddled downstairs and out the door
into a summer evening, while
you and mother ate spaghetti
on the porch. If it's true,
I don't remember the room I thought
to escape. Floating about that tiny
house in a doze, I can still see
the goldfish idling in a bowl near
the window, the alphabet blocks
strewn across the rug, but when
it comes to climbing stairs,
or opening any of several doors,
the dream goes dark. Not just
forgotten, almost forbidden.

I've learned to live in peace
with whatever memory grants
or withholds, learned to love
its clumsy reconstructions,
how easily it adopts a fiction
as its own, as a tributary
to the heart. In this way living
with the past is like living
by an ideal, unsure if it is true
sometimes, or if it matters.
In Saint-Exupéry's *Night Flight*
the philosophical Rivière says—
We don't ask to live forever,
only that what we live by never seems
a fraud. I have lived by this tale,
father, and haven't the courage
to ask you if it's true. Each time
I go back I find the world sealed
off behind me. Evening is opening
over the trees, salmon and silver.
A young man walks his son along a road
that still smells of tar at its soft
borders, past the pitiful pairs
of saplings in each identical yard,
toward the bare frames of split-levels,
and the muddy tractor ruts where
the road leaves off. From behind
a grove of pines comes the blast
of an engine. The man stops to listen,
then hoists the child up, throws him
across his shoulder and begins to run.

They cross a footbridge and some
woods, and the man sets the child down
in my life, in the soft brown needles
at the meadow's edge. The biplane
trundles past so close my blood
trembles, the rudder swinging
and all the clover rippling
in its wake. We stood waving, father,
until the plane turned and rolled
toward the far end of that field
where my life began twenty-three
years ago. And I wonder now,
watching those wings strive up again
over the trees, unsteady at first,
what's gained by knowing we really saw it.
Not even your astonished smile
could tell me that—the field is full
of houses now. The plane cleared the trees
and was gone.

Blaming the Swan

Everywhere you look the landscape
fails you, divides you, demands
a quality of remorse you cannot
summon yet. Even here, in the dark
preserve at the center of town,
their faces swim out of moonlight's
scribble on the pond: pumpkin
smashers, petty thieves, torturers
of cats, and those in whom violence
slept more deeply. Nothing can
console the boy you watched beat
Grogan's thicklipped brother because
he wanted a little silence, or
the simian one who brained his grandmother
with a wrench. They are altogether beyond
forgiveness now, will never get free
of the deadly winch at the center
of their lives, because you cannot
let them, because you can feel,
in the swan's wake drawing like
a bowstring across the pond, how your own
proud heart might someday come to painful
poise, just as a whole moon like this
floats up behind the trees.

Homecoming

The bedroom I unpack in seems smaller with each visit,
pressed by the waves descending the windows.
The bluff has been cleared of Japanese rose,
bramble and thistle, the elms are gone,
and a garden uses the old field we played on.
I don't begrudge the view.
The channel bells still beat beneath our sleep.
Downstairs grandmother puts the past in order,
piling a table with ragged editions of St. Nicholas,
open to essays on jug fishing or the founding of Danzig.

Other things are not so well in hand.
I find the icebox full of rotten bowls,
a cake as a pale green pavilion of mold.
We sit for coffee and the old clock leaves
its soft signature on the air. Rolling newsprint
to kindle, I read about the world as it was.
My family still reads under the same three lamps.
I still make the fire with driftwood and cedar,
hoping for jets of green and bluish flame,
but these evenings have assumed the look of tableaux—
the sound of a spoon in a cup seals us in.
When the fire inflates they look up and smile.
Their glasses flare with the light.

This afternoon I watched ragged chevrons of geese
veer south, and at evening stood the telescope
in the dry leaves out back. Across the bay I zeroed in
the amusement park. The red ferris wheel revolved,
revolved, upside down in the lens, a tiny gear
that seemed to work at spinning the whole earth very slowly.

Every journey out and back I make describes an horizon.
Though married and moved away, I keep returning,
as if some night beside the bedroom window
that leaks the southwest wind and the mutter of surf,
I could explain my life. The small skull of my car
follows the peninsula, the sea dark on both sides,
down the path where she coaxed holly to grow
in beds of coffee grounds and tea leaves,
out of its latitude.

The Whale

for my sister

There is only one letter I should have written you
and it isn't this. It should have arrived from Norway
the summer you and father circled under the birdie,
racquets poised, or come one bleak afternoon while mother
talked on into the phone. Your face rose in the window
to watch the squirrels pray on the feeder.
Every day for years they came edging along the sash,
quizzical, tails pressed against the glass.

For years I didn't believe in this kind of sadness—
never imagined the small nights in your bedroom,
the mirrors in which you were always disappointing yourself.
Have you ever slipped into the guest-room
where father slept alone for so many years, looking
for some trace of his private life, and found in a drawer
a murder mystery—on the cover someone fending off her fate
with a gloved arm and a long voiceless scream?

I know how you loved him but wouldn't say so,
standing on the edge of the Cape Cod Canal with the high
rusty sides of a freighter passing, the huge prop
threshing the water white. I know how sorry you were for him
that there were no fish in the ponds you both cast into,
that the camera sank when he capsized the weekend dinghy.
When you got home the racoons had already climbed
to mother's window to wash and feed on stale doughnuts.
Through the bedroom door you heard her talk to them,
and their claws on the roof crept in and out of your sleep.

So you see how close I think I come to this—
the assumption of our life. Sometimes late at night
I turn a page and what I see through the page
is what we have not yet given each other.
We both have seen mother set a glass of scotch
on the piano, and heard Gershwin and Debussy seep up
through the floor. What I meant to tell you in the letter
I never wrote was about how large life can grow.
It is ten P.M., sundown, and I'm sailing home
on the smooth fjord, when it broaches five yards away—
a hump of black silk, a shot of steam, and the great flukes
slicing back under the surface.

Sestina

for Egil

Today my insides swerve like a school of fish
when I think of the self-devotions by the water,
or run across those paltry sketches of darkness
as it fell over the mountains without stars.
There is one, in pencil, of a mackerel before it reached the fire.
In the purse of its mouth sleep all the forgotten names:

the shepherd's tall green island the Nazis renamed,
the words for turnip, gravestones, lavender moss, the inlet fished
out and full of reeds, the beer we drank in silence by fires
on the beach, what you called the shepherd's daughter's hair, water
caught in pools, but most of all the names of fish fit only to fade
    like stars
into the deep where the creatures feed in darkness.

We tended the lines until morning melted the darkness,
taught each other shreds of crude invective, the names
in our two tongues of shapes that rose from the star-
flecked swells, cut our fingers on the gills of fish
I didn't recognize. At home we cleaned and rinsed the catch in
    water.
You dared me to eat a fish heart, laughed, and went on building
    the fire.

The white flesh fell from the bones and brandy fired
our family gatherings. Gradually the conversation left me in the
    dark,
and after dinner, full of my own language, I'd walk down to the
    water
that had fallen twelve feet from the shaggy rocks, and name
everything around me in a whisper, throwing fish-
heads from a bucket to the gulls, imagining I was alone under the
    stars.

I thought of Thoreau, casting his line out into the stars
in a solitude like vertigo, of how love is like a fire
built and rebuilt on the same hearth, how the fish
are anonymous and capable in their world. At last all the windows
     darkened.
I remember little more of that summer ten years back; the names
of all the strangers I met and misunderstood have vanished in those
     waters.

But today I read that the trawlers find little in the water
but what was once considered trash—pout, snook, gag, ratfish—stars
in an aquatic burlesque, their sweet flesh maligned because of their
     names.
An advertising agency is making them new titles, so as not to fire
the diner's imagination. Why not? No one knows what hungers in
     the dark
among the fins. But time and seasoning can flatter the ugliest fish

that's harbored in memory. Boiling water or a slow fire—
I've grown catholic in my tastes. I take whatever regrets the stars
     or darkness
give me back, and forgive us both the neglected names of fish.

Sketch

Holding a picture up to the wall,
I look beyond your arms folded
and head cocked in appraisal to the window.
The wind's eye distinguishes nothing
out of the ordinary, but the leaves poise

like a nervous glade of bows before
the conductor dips his baton. All
our gestures begin their comforting
cadences again. Roasting smells
rise upstairs and linger.

Across the street a woman steps out
of her slack-spined house with a brood
of mottled cats, the same woman
who said to me—I don't know
where you've come from, Chicago

or wherever, but your dog has to be
on a leash. Now I realize that we
could have come here from anywhere,
not just the years we've lived together
listening in town after town to cars

accelerate uphill, trailing familiar
flags of music from their windows.
Perhaps this is only a way of ignoring
what was said about the leash,
but I think not. Standing together

watching sunset burnish a sliver of lake
hung in the leaves, we belong in our
life again. Dozens of windows flicker
in the valley. You seem to have just fallen
into my heart at its dusk.

Music for Piano and Electrical Storm

After a twilight walk I climb the stairs,
lie down and trace the muscles of your thighs,
from the boyish knees to the perfectly pale
flanks that shine upon the sheets.
Outside the light is failing early,
and in tall cumulus lightning decides
what has ranged too far from the earth's
elaborate surface: a steeple, a tree, a man walking home
alone through an indolent yellow field.

In the heat my body listens to itself,
hears with inexplicable pleasure the past walking
softly but deliberately away,
like the right hand up a keyboard diminuendo.
Even as it desires comfort, when it would call back
all that it loved, the body craves an absence
of its own. Sometimes after driving hours
in calm silence beside you,
I have looked out into the pines across a shallow river
and imagined a glade where I could fall asleep forever,
where nothing I touched would pretend to be understood.
There I'd feed every cell of this flesh
to the wind that smells of cedar and of smoke.

The first ragged thrusts of light
loose in the sky an instant leave us
in greater darkness. I would call you back
from dreams, but know better. So I turn my love
on you, too gently to wake you, expecting nothing,
like one who is grateful years later
for the sad nocturne a stranger played
in an open summer house he passed one night.

Your eyes don't even tremble
when the lightning flares,
but I know your skin goes white
where it's touched.
This is what is meant by calling. Station to station.

Rain unravels across the window, and all the nights
I've stared out into rain come back to compose this roof,
this bed, as surely as they compose my breathing.
I remember how the rain worked on me,
when I moved into the bed's cold frontier alone
and watched the trees shudder, all of what was invisible
visible in their flourishes and sway. Like wind
something within yearns without flesh or words
to mask it. Even the gods were uneasy
in their costumes of muscle and nerve.
Tempted flesh betrayed them, be they bull or swan
or laurel in their love. Suppose the cedars
flared up blue in a moonlit meadow—
they'd never know how the chosen's tears
made them flicker.

This is what is meant by calling—
a voice spent on silence while the rain subsides.

Each white fingerprint I leave on your thigh
fades like a pedalled note from a piano.

I would call back what I loved.

Elegy

A thousand miles of seaboard are closing
down tonight, as we drive north hour by hour.
The lights begin to vanish from Maryland
truck farms, moored across acres of sour
stubble. Refineries loom on the dark
marshes, lit up like cruise ships for evening
watch, and radio towers softly spark
on the windshield. Tonight I think of them as
the tall stakes of fogbound weirs contrived
to net the invisible in their migrations.
The world has ceased revolving in you, but we
don't nearly understand this; we must arrive.

I remember that your frail body will
not be left to us to bury—nothing
of you would be wasted if study could fulfill
another's dream of continuing life.
As I hold my wife's hand this seems at first
a horror, and then an act of faith
that places you more certainly in a world
I must rediscover, because love
will not accept the thought of darkness
continuing darkness. When I'd phone you
on dull evenings, you'd confess
to fatigue, but you were always "so's to be up and about."

That phrase lingers with me now and lights
our way home. Rudiments we learned
as children of the physics
of the spirit, its release and its flights
among the living—these I remember now
and fiercely believe. And though
I can imagine your skeptical smile, I wonder
how should we speak to what lingers of you
in the old seaside house. After a day
under sail I remember mysterious swells
still seeming to rise under our chairs at dinner, and bells
that after months inland, persisted in my sleep.

You'd wait for us there by the sea. Now we come
this last time to you. I cannot decide
about death, or the lights that pinwheel
in my eyes—how best to respond
to either. No one knows, not those intimate
to me, nor those in the crowd of headlights
in the mirror. But the mile-a-minute
pace we take to your silence tonight
unfurls some of the distance I am to discover
with the name you trusted me.
I inch a finger over the map,
where my heart and I must settle together one day.

for Elizabeth M. Farnsworth
1900–1978

A Lover's Quarrel with the World

High summer sunset. A solitary hornet climbs
slowly over all the softening peaches on the porch.
Beneath the whitewashed bench a pile of shells—
bleached impasto hulls, cloudy violet inside,
the salt-crusted gritty sneakers tenderfoot guests
were given for swimming, scraps of green seaglass.
Left alone, thoughts opened more slowly
than the tiger lilies on the bluff, breathing
like the bellied screens in the southwest wind
that drove the yachts home, yawning like lungs
that would consume everything and themselves,
leaving just sunset, stones cooling
on the beach, shreds of music from a passing boat,
the gulls.
               Sitting up inland late by this frozen
window, I want words about transparency, the thin
film of tears sheathing the eye, cold water wrinkling
over perfectly motionless stones, memory's unavoidable
transpositions. I would ask again, as once
beneath a streetlamp rain caught on my glasses
revealed a dozen spiralling cells—how can the world
have so many centers and cohere? I would ask
for another evening on that porch, hoping
that if I faced again the beaten silver of the sea
at sundown, I could at last speak for my life,
including at once the immeasurable flutter of hornet
wings, and the vast sidereal motion of the stars.

It is foolish to talk like this, I know.
If the present is sparrows lighting on a telephone wire
that is full of regrettable talk, or clouds
at the window claiming to have changed the lives
of grains and philosophers a thousand miles west,
then it is true, all true, what happened and what
we dreamed of it—there is no source to be discovered.

There is only the light, born or captured here,
only the shadows' vague inscriptions.

I have spent the evening staring at the paintings
of Vermeer. Looking at all that north light aslant
through the same leaded window, on a woman reading
a letter or pouring milk, you could almost believe
in mercy. Nearly all his work was done in one house
in Delft, and done for the love of pure vision alone,
each scene given its own peculiar stillness
so that ordinary afternoons belonged without presumption
to eternity. It is not at all what is seen
or remembered, but how one manages the act
of vision itself, how to contain the moment;
the woman's letter or the fastidious hornet,
and also the spare music of a life winding
down. It is there, in the light.

The red house down the street was winched
from its foundation three blocks away and
hauled to the empty lot where we had always
parked our car. For months I've been thinking
of the new light falling in each of its rooms,
how subtly and irrevocably its inhabitants'
lives have changed. It is not simply loss
that divides us from things, nor the desire
implicit in reflection.
              I could go back
to that porch in August, and wait again
for someone to come watch with me thin cirrus
crafting the bright air. I can bite into
the velvet skin of a peach and throw the glistening
stone into the woods. I can promise myself I will;
I can say that I have. I haven't.

I have trusted my life to this language,
every moment given to argument or love—
as water argues with sunlight, as the mirror,
hung at a slight angle from the wall,
calmly tilts this room toward the window:
the glossy headboard, green quilt, the blank white
wall relieved by the painting I took down one night
in my sleep, seeking a view where there was none
before. Such trust I place in these rooms,
and in the rooms that preceded them. It is enough
to say I am responsible for all I've neglected
to remember or imagine.

The wind continues sculpting the snow on the roof,
while downstairs the tap water my wife runs
for coffee changes tone as it changes temperature.
From the foot of the stairs next door my neighbor
calls to her niece—turn out your light, you can
read some more tomorrow. From the dark ridge
beyond town, across the frozen lake, a stream
of headlights snakes down, each pair miraculously
appearing from what seems to be the sky.

In the houses these people approach or
depart, the darkness persists without
interference, and somewhere in the old
world, an observatory's white shell
slides gravely open, and the great lens
focuses once more on the bright whirl of dust
it's been tracking all these years across the sky.